For the little people who encourage us to roar like dinosaurs,
walk like crabs, and sing silly songs about EVERYTHING.

For Mum, Dad, Katie, and Sam - For accepting me at
my worst whilst encouraging me to be my best.

For TJ, who will never know the impact
he had on my life and my heart.

Text copyright @ 2024 Estelle Brandreth

Illustrations copyright @ 2024 Daisy Hope Birchenough

The right of Estelle Brandreth and Daisy Hope Birchenough to be identified as the author
and illustrator of this work has been asserted by them in accordance with
the Copyright, Designs and Patents Act 1988.

All rights reserved, including the right of reproduction in whole or in part, in any form.

ISBN: 9798883054296

TJ! No!

Written by Estelle Brandreth
Illustrated by Daisy Hope Birchenough

TJ is a naughty cat, a playful little soul.
Mess is his mission, and mischief is his goal.

He jumped onto the windowsill, and lifted up his paws.

I saw that he was going to scratch the curtains with his claws!

He's going to rip the curtains if I don't let him know.
So, I bellowed from across the room...

TJ! No!

He ran his claws from top to bottom,
leaving holes for all to see.

Then he jumped down,
and walked away,
and left the mess for me.

I looked out of the window
and saw TJ starting to creep.
Hidden in the grass,
wiggling his tail, about to leap.

I looked across the garden
and I saw a little bird.
Unaware of TJ, who she hadn't
seen or heard.

He's going to hurt the bird, that poor little sparrow,
So, I bellowed from the window...

TJ! No!

He looked at me,

then looked away,

and then he did it
anyway!

He sprung to life,
and pounced towards
that poor little bird.

Thankfully, she flew away
but still TJ purred.

Even though he hadn't managed to make the bird his dinner,

he had scared the silly bird, so he still felt like a winner!

Sat at the dining room table, with a jigsaw puzzle to complete,
I suddenly heard the pitter-patter of naughty little feet.

TJ strolled across the table, and to my horror I saw, one of my jigsaw puzzle pieces stuck to his little paw!

He's going to lose the puzzle piece, if I let him go,
So, I bellowed from the table...

TJ! No!

He looked at me,

then looked away,

and then he did it
anyway!

Quick as a flash, he left the room,
before he could release,

the item stuck to his paw,
my missing puzzle piece!

My neighbour takes great pride in their garden, they water it a lot!

So, imagine the panic when I saw TJ, climbing into their plant pot.

He's going to ruin the flowers
that they've worked so hard to grow!
So, I bellowed over the fence...

TJ! No!

He looked at me,

then looked away,

and then he did it **anyway!**

He jumped into the plant pot,
squashing the flowers flat.

Then he turned around
to get comfortable,
and then he finally sat.

He eventually jumped out,
when he heard me shouting

"SHOO!"

He saw that I was cross,
so he did it quickly too!

I have a glass vase, sat up on the side,
with a beautiful bunch of flowers,
arranged nicely inside.

Out the corner of my eye,
I could see TJ sat up on the ledge,

pushing the vase with one little paw,
slowly towards the edge.

Just a few more shoves, and that vase will smash below.
So, I bellowed from across the room...

He pushed the vase until it fell,
smashing on the floor,

then he jumped over the mess he'd made
and scarpered out the door.

Lying in my bed, in the middle of the night,
I felt footsteps on the bed, so I turned on the light.

There was TJ, purring loudly,
he pressed his nose against mine,

then curled up next to me,
and we both knew all was fine.

Because no matter how naughty he is,
and no matter how much mess,
if he asks for a cuddle, the answer is...

TJ! Yes!

Printed in Great Britain
by Amazon